TINTIN'S TRAVEL DIARIES

Publisher's note:

Tintin, the intrepid reporter, first made his appearance January 10, 1929, in a serial newspaper strip with an adventure in the Soviet Union. From there, it was on to the Belgian Congo and then to America. Together with his dog Snowy; an old seaman, Captain Haddock; an eccentric professor, Cuthbert Calculus: look-alike detectives, Thomson and Thompson; and others, Tintin roamed the world from one adventure to the next.

Tintin's dog, Snowy, a small white fox terrier, converses with Tintin, saves his life many times, and acts as his confidant, despite his weakness far whiskey and a tendency toward greediness. Captain Haddock, in some ways Snowy's counterpart, is a reformed lover of whiskey, with a tendency toward colorful language and a desire to be a gentleman-farmer. Cuthbert Calculus, a hard-of-hearing, sentimental, absent-minded professor, goes from small-time inventor to nuclear physicist. The detectives, Thomson and Thompson, stereotyped characters down to their old-fashioned bowler hats and outdated expressions, are always chasing Tintin. Their attempts at dressing in the costume of the place they are in make them stand out all the more.

The Adventures of Tintin appeared in newspapers and books all over the world. Georges Remi (1907–1983), better known as Hergé, based Tintin's adventures on his own interest in and knowledge of places around the world. The stories were often irreverent, frequently political and satirical, and always exciting and humorous.

Tintin's Travel Diaries is a new series, inspired by Hergé's characters and based on notebooks Tintin may have kept as he traveled. Each book in this series takes the reader to a different country, exploring its geography, and the customs, the culture, and the heritage of the people living there. Hergé's original cartooning is used, juxtaposed with photographs showing the country as it is today, to give a feeling of fun as well as education.

If Herge's cartoons seem somewhat out of place in today's society, think of the time in which they were drawn. The cartoons reflect the thinking of the day, and set next to modern photographs, we learn something about ourselves and society, as well as about the countries Tintin explores. We can see how attitudes have changed over the course of half a century.

Hergé, himself, would change his stories and drawings periodically to reflect the changes in society and the comments his work would receive. For example, when it was originally written in 1930, *Tintin in the Congo,* on which *Tintin's Travel Diaries: Africa* is based, was slanted toward Belgium as the fatherland. When Hergé prepared a color version in 1946, he did away with this slant. Were Hergé alive today, he would probably change many other stereotypes that appear in his work.

From the Congo, Tintin went on to America. This was in 1931. Al Capone was notorious, and the idea of cowboys and Indians, prohibition, the wild west, as well as factories, all held a place of fascination. *Cigars of the Pharaoh* (1934) introduced Hergé's fans to the mysteries of Egypt and India. A trip to China came with *The Blue Lotus* in 1936, the first story Hergé thoroughly researched. After that, everything was researched, including revisions of previous stories. The *Land of Black Gold,* for example, an adventure in the Middle East, was written in 1939, and revised in 1949 and again in 1969.

Although *The Broken Ear* introduced readers to the Amazon region in 1935, the story was pure fantasy, complete with imaginary countries. In 1974 the adventure continued with *Tintin and the Picaros,* Hergé's last story. When *The Seven Crystal Balls,* which was serialized from 1943 to 1944, was continued in 1946, Hergé began to give the reader factual information about pre-Columbian civilization with marginal notes titled "Who were the Incas?" Tintin in the land of the Soviets was Tintin's first adventure, in 1929, and the only one not to be redone in color.

Tintin's Travel Diaries are fun to read, fun to look at, and provide educational, enjoyable trips around the world. Perhaps, like Tintin, you, too, will be inspired to seek out new adventures!

The publisher particularly wishes to thank Mrs. Christine Ockrent and television channel Antenne 2 for their kind permission to use the title *Travel Diaries.*

EGYPT
AND THE MIDDLE EAST

TINTIN'S TRAVEL DIARIES

A collection conceived and produced by Martine Noblet.

Les films du sable thank the following **Connaissance du monde** photographers for their participation in this work:

Christian Monty, Paul Jacques Callebaut, Alain Saint-Hilaire, Olivier Berthelot, Jacques Cornet.

The authors thank M. Chauvet, C. Deltenre, and Christiane Erard for their collaboration.

First edition for the United States and Canada published by Barron's Educational Series, Inc., 1995.

All inquiries should be addressed to:
Barron's Educational Series, Inc.
250 Wireless Boulevard
Hauppauge, New York 11788

Library of Congress Catalog Card No.: 94-37088

International Standard Book No. 0-8120-6488-7 (hard cover)
International Standard Book No. 0-8120-9159-0 (paperback)

Library of Congress Cataloging-in-Publication Data
Bruycker, Daniel de.
    [Egypte et le Moyen-Orient. English]
    Egypt and the Middle East / text by Daniel De Bruycker and Maximilien
Dauber ; translation by Maureen Walker.
        p.   cm. — (Tintin's travel diaries)
    Includes bibliographical references and index.
    ISBN 0-8120-6488-7. — ISBN 0-8120-9159-0 (pbk.)
    1. Egypt — Description and travel — Juvenile literature.
I. Dauber, Maximilien. II. Title. III. Series.
DT56.2B7813 1995   94-37088
962—dc20   CIP
                                                                          AC

Printed in Hong Kong
5678   9927   987654321

EGYPT
AND THE MIDDLE EAST

Text by Daniel De Bruycker and Maximilien Dauber

Translation by Maureen Walker

BARRON'S

Tintin is the same age as I am. I grew up with him, but he hasn't aged. I got to know him during World War II, when the evenings were long and cold. We had our heroes to warm our hearts: Tintin, Tarzan, Mickey Mouse, and the rest.

I wasn't one of the heroes, but like every boy my age, I longed to be one. Tintin accomplished great deeds in my place. He opened up for me worlds that I was hardly able to imagine and that we talked about with bated breath: the Belgian Congo, from which quite often some relative failed to return; the Egypt of the pharaohs that my teacher used to talk about in history lessons; and America, whose aircraft we watched passing overhead. It all mixed adventure and freedom. Since then, I've walked in the footsteps of my hero, and I think I would feel very sad if I were to forget him.

PAUL-JACQUES CALLEBAUT

The old "magic lantern" slide projector at the boys' club of a Paris church introduced me, in black and white, to Tintin. My imagination got a good workout. Week after week I looked forward to the adventures of the astute reporter, a brilliant problem-solver, so resourceful, bringing to life a world reflecting his time.

The death of the cartoonist who created him froze Tintin forever in this adventure series. Yet Tintin is ageless. There is not the slightest doubt that he could have continued his story in today's world with the same verve and zest, for Tintin is not, and never was, nostalgic for the past. I am all the more sure of it because many years afterward, in Arabia and the Middle East, I met the people with whom he had lived. Like him, I was fascinated by the mystery of Tutankhamen's treasure, the practical jokes of the "black and gold" princes, and in a more serious vein, by the political-religious conflicts that disturb the Middle East.

ALAIN SAINT-HILAIRE

CONTENTS

The words in **boldface** refer to the glossary beginning on page 70.

WHY IS EGYPT CALLED "THE GIFT OF THE NILE"?

Egypt contains two distinct kinds of land areas that are very different from each other. The first, much larger than Texas, is an uninhabited desert. The other is a long strip of fertile land, the Valley of the Nile, where most Egyptians live.

S urrounded by the vast barren spaces of the Sahara, Egypt is more part of the East and the Mediterranean world than of Africa. The famous "fertile crescent," which in ancient times was the cradle of the first western civilizations, extended from the banks of the Nile to **Mesopotamia.** Thus Egypt is the size of Texas, Oklahoma, and Arkansas combined.

Without the Nile, which runs 1,000 miles (1,600 km) through Egypt, Egypt could never have supported a sedentary population: The climate is blazing hot and rain is almost nonexistent. Every year for thousands of years, the river, swollen by the rains of central Africa, overflowed, flooding it entire valley. As a result, it deeply watered the soil before subsiding, leaving behind a layer of fertile mud, called silt. The early Egyptians learned how to channel the overflows to save part of the floodwater. As early as the time of the pharaohs, a canal emptied into Lake Fayyum, near Cairo. But the river controlled the fate of the Egyptians, who were at the mercy of floods that were sometimes too little, sometimes too abundant.

Since 1964, the waters of the Nile have been controlled upstream by the colossal **Aswan High Dam,** which redistributes water all year long for irrigation. Unfortunately the dam also holds back the fertilizing muds that the river used to carry, and the soil is gradually becoming poor, forcing the peasants to use chemical fertilizers.

Top: A type of sailing ship called a "felucca," in the Upper Nubian Valley
Bottom: A fellah (Egyptian peasant)

WHO ARE THE FELLAHIN?

The fellahin are peasants who, in ancient times, made up most of Egypt's population. Today over half of more than 57 million Egyptians live in the countryside.

The fellahin still look like their distant ancestors, whose figures adorn the walls of temples and tombs of ancient Egypt. Their way of life has hardly changed either. Today, as it was 5,000 years ago, the fellah is still a poor peasant, renting a scrap of land that is farmed according to ancestral methods. He has hardly enough left to feed his family once the landowner has collected a portion, often a large one, of the cotton, sugarcane, rice, corn, or wheat harvest. Unable to buy modern farming machinery to lighten his work and improve the yield of his fields, he therefore finds it difficult to provide a better education for his children, who are in danger of being condemned in their turn to live in this precarious way.

The future of the Egyptian peasant is all the more diffi-cult because in one century the country's population has multiplied by eight and is continuing to increase rapidly. The lack of habitable land forces many peasants to leave the countryside and swell the population of cities that are already overcrowded. Greater Cairo has about 10 million inhabi-tants, and the housing shortage is so severe that some people have had to settle in the district of the old cemeteries, in an area known as the City of the Dead.

Left: A peasant working in the fields
Right: A sheik (tribal leader)

WHO WERE THE PHARAOHS?

For the ancient Egyptians, the ruling pharaoh was a god, a child of the sun god. After his death, he went to join the other gods, masters of the universe, while his son or designated successor became the next head of Egypt.

Around 3100 B.C., the small kingdoms scattered along the banks of the Nile joined together as one nation, under the authority of the first king of the first of Egypt's thirty-one dynasties. From Narmer (or Menes) to Nectanebo, with the most famous of the **pharaohs** on the way—Khufu, Thutmose III, Amenhotep IV (later known as Akhenaton), Tutankhamen, Ramses II, and the queens **Hatshepsut** and **Nefertiti**—as much time elapsed as between the founding of Rome and today....

These great sovereigns left behind some impressive monuments, huge tombs and temples, flanked by **obelisks**. Since ancient times, their capital cities, starting with Memphis (near Cairo), then Thebes (which later became Luxor), have astonished travelers with the grandeur and harmony of their architecture, as have the colossal statues that stand guard on the banks of the Nile, or the fantastic pyramids that still capture the imagination.

But the long history of this great nation is full of disturbances, too—conquests and defeats, confrontations between Upper Egypt, south of the Nile delta, and Lower Egypt, in the river's delta. There were many traitors and usurpers who incited palace intrigues, set against a background of fierce struggles between the pharaohs and their priestly followers.

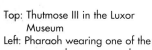

Top: Thutmose III in the Luxor Museum
Left: Pharaoh wearing one of the crowns, the *nemes,* and, on his chest, the scepter called the *heka* (Dynasty XVIII)
Right: The head of Akhenaton

WHAT WAS THE FUNCTION OF A PYRAMID?

During the earliest dynasties, the Egyptians wondered what would become of their souls after death. From the pyramids of Giza to the tombs in the Valley of the Kings to the ancient temples at Thebes, the most famous monuments are first and foremost tombs.

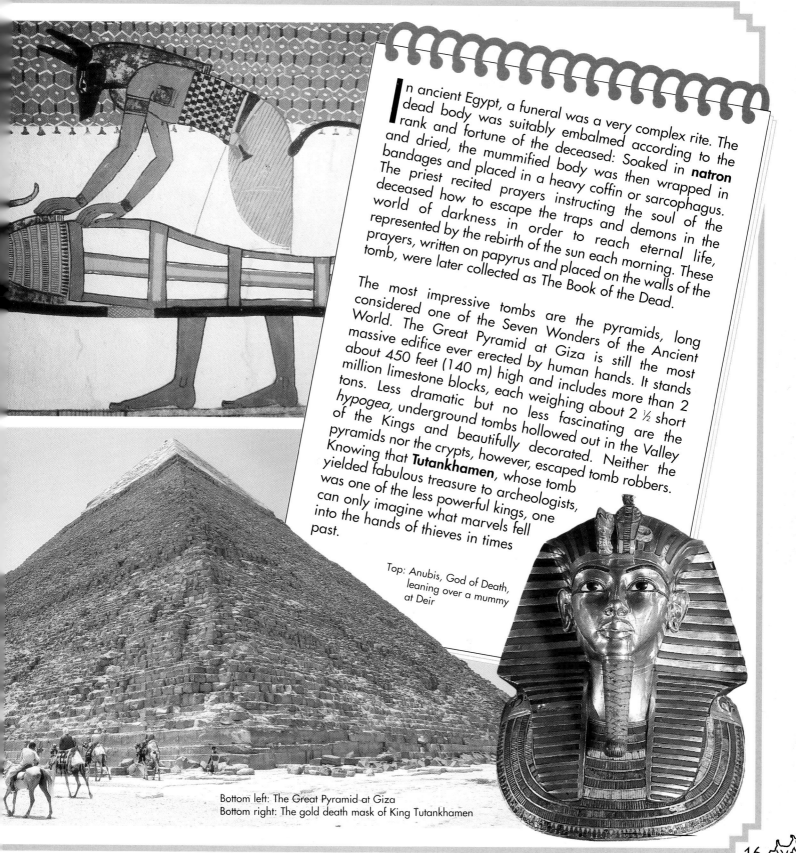

In ancient Egypt, a funeral was a very complex rite. The dead body was suitably embalmed according to the rank and fortune of the deceased: Soaked in **natron** and dried, the mummified body was then wrapped in bandages and placed in a heavy coffin or sarcophagus. The priest recited prayers instructing the soul of the deceased how to escape the traps and demons in the world of darkness in order to reach eternal life, represented by the rebirth of the sun each morning. These prayers, written on papyrus and placed on the walls of the tomb, were later collected as The Book of the Dead.

The most impressive tombs are the pyramids, long considered one of the Seven Wonders of the Ancient World. The Great Pyramid at Giza is still the most massive edifice ever erected by human hands. It stands about 450 feet (140 m) high and includes more than 2 million limestone blocks, each weighing about 2 ½ short tons. Less dramatic but no less fascinating are the hypogea, underground tombs hollowed out in the Valley of the Kings and beautifully decorated. Neither the pyramids nor the crypts, however, escaped tomb robbers. Knowing that **Tutankhamen**, whose tomb yielded fabulous treasure to archeologists, was one of the less powerful kings, one can only imagine what marvels fell into the hands of thieves in times past.

Top: Anubis, God of Death, leaning over a mummy at Deir

Bottom left: The Great Pyramid at Giza
Bottom right: The gold death mask of King Tutankhamen

WHAT IS A HIEROGLYPH?

Hieroglyphs, or "temple drawings," are one of the earliest forms of writing known. They are pictures and symbols put together to represent objects, ideas, people, or actions from the everyday lives of the Egyptians.

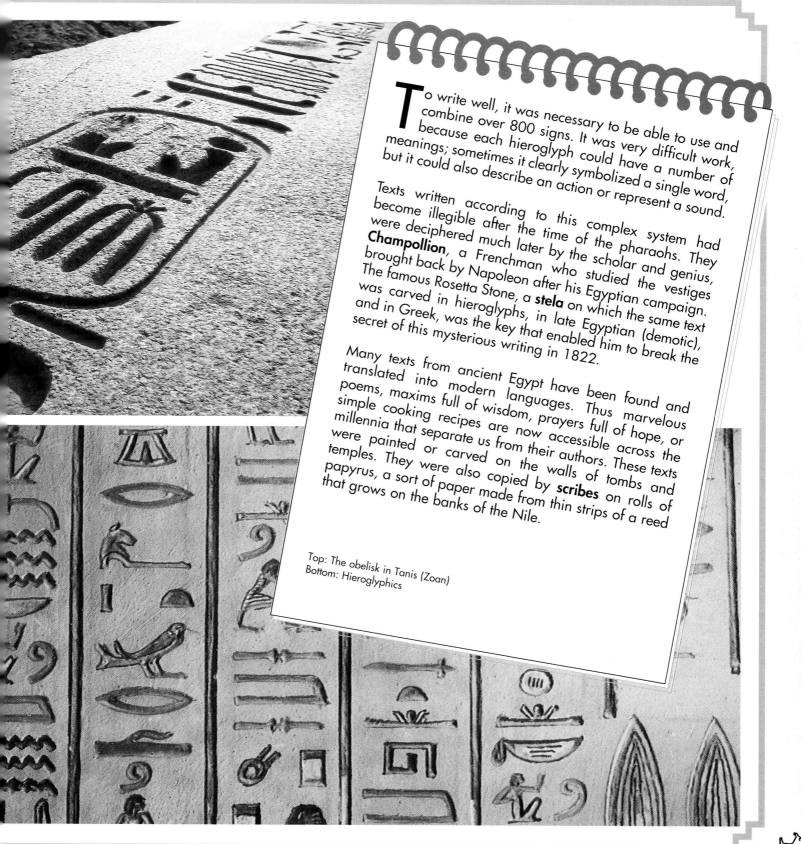

To write well, it was necessary to be able to use and combine over 800 signs. It was very difficult work, because each hieroglyph could have a number of meanings; sometimes it clearly symbolized a single word, but it could also describe an action or represent a sound.

Texts written according to this complex system had become illegible after the time of the pharaohs. They were deciphered much later by the scholar and genius, **Champollion**, a Frenchman who studied the vestiges brought back by Napoleon after his Egyptian campaign. The famous Rosetta Stone, a **stela** on which the same text was carved in hieroglyphs, in late Egyptian (demotic), and in Greek, was the key that enabled him to break the secret of this mysterious writing in 1822.

Many texts from ancient Egypt have been found and translated into modern languages. Thus marvelous poems, maxims full of wisdom, prayers full of hope, or simple cooking recipes are now accessible across the millennia that separate us from their authors. These texts were painted or carved on the walls of tombs and temples. They were also copied by **scribes** on rolls of papyrus, a sort of paper made from thin strips of a reed that grows on the banks of the Nile.

Top: The obelisk in Tanis (Zoan)
Bottom: Hieroglyphics

HOW DO WE KNOW SO MUCH ABOUT ANCIENT EGYPT?

We are quite well informed about the Egyptians of antiquity thanks to their writings, the objects that they buried with their dead, the sculptures, and the frescoes decorating temples and tombs.

Everyday objects, such as vases and furniture, placed in Egyptian tombs, and the painted pictures of everyday life were intended to provide the deceased with the things that had surrounded him during his life that he would need for his existence in the "other world." It is easy to recognize domestic activities, agricultural tools, and crop plants, especially since nearly all of them still exist in Egypt today.

In the temples, pictures of the gods were often placed next to those of the pharoahs, glorifying their battle scenes. The gods are usually represented with an animal's head: a falcon for Horus, a jackal for Anubis, an ibis for Thoth, and a crocodile for Sobek. Such animals, dedicated to the gods, were honored and even embalmed.

Among the most important divinities, the sun god Re', later called Amon-Re', was the proctector of the pharaohs. Then came Nut, goddess of the sky; Isis, protectress of mothers and children; and Osiris, the god of the dead. In the sanctuaries, a multitude of priests were very influential in Egyptian society because of their knowledge, as scribes, physicians, astronomers, architects, or embalmers.

Left: Anubis, God of Death
Right: Bas-relief and hieroglyphics on the tomb of Ramose (Thebes)

WHO WERE THE FIRST EGYPTOLOGISTS?

Greek scholars were passionately interested in the prestigious monuments of Egyptian civilization, but it was not until the nineteenth century with Champollion and Mariette, that the study of ancient Egypt became a real science.

Egyptology is not an easy job. Many monuments, if not engulfed by sand, have been damaged by earthquakes or destructive actions of the Egyptians themselves. Moreover, in the nineteenth century a number of relics, sometimes weighing dozens of tons, were dismantled and hauled away to decorate museums or city squares in the great European capitals.

The unflagging zeal of tomb robbers complicates the study, too. Already very active in the time of the pharaohs, they dodged the guards assigned to grave protection in order to snatch finely worked pieces of gold jewelry and melt them down into ordinary ingots that were easier to sell. Even today, trafficking in antiques is sustained by unscrupulous collectors, and is considered alarming by researchers and the nation as a whole.

But the biggest challenge Egyptologists encountered was the construction of the Aswan High Dam, whose retaining Lake Nasser ended up engulfing some of the most prestigious remains from the time of the pharaohs. Scholars from all over the world joined together, under the auspices of **UNESCO**, to save the principal monuments from destruction. In the case of the Island of Philae or the colossal temples of Abu Simbel, hundreds of millions of tons of rock had to be removed from their pedestals, then transported and reassembled higher up on the banks of the new lake.

Top: Explorers Cailliaud and Letorzec in the Nubian Valley
Bottom: The stone colossus on Tumbus Island

HOW DID ALEXANDRIA GET ITS NAME?

Alexander the Great, King of Macedonia, put an end to the power of the pharaohs in 332 B.C. and founded a new capital in the Nile delta, Alexandria. It remains the second most important city in Egypt today.

While the ancient cities built by the pharaohs were declining, Alexandria became, in the time of the Greeks and then of the Romans, the world center for science and culture. In its famous library, the richest one of its time, scholars like Euclid (the founder of geometry), and the first Christian philosophers used to study.

This intellectual life flourished in a city that was very active in trade. The famous Pharos tower, one of the Seven Wonders of the Ancient World, was topped by a light at night and guided vessels safely into port. From its name was derived the word "phare," French for "lighthouse."

Looting, the fire at the great library, and the Arab invasion put an end to this glorious period. But in the nineteenth century, under the influence of the viceroy, Muhammad Ali, Alexandria emerged from a sleep that had lasted over 1,000 years to become once again Egypt's chief port and an important trading metropolis. Asians and Europeans both shared the prosperity engendered by opening the Suez Canal, which connects the Mediterranean to the Red Sea, thereby avoiding sailing around the tip of Africa. Even today, so many years after it was constructed by Ferdinand de Lesseps in 1869, this strategic waterway gives Egypt an important status in world maritime traffic.

Alexandria, which enjoys a moister, cooler climate than the rest of the country, is also the favorite seaside resort of the Egyptians, who relax on its beaches and in its casinos and nightclubs.

Top: The entrance to port of Alexandria   Bottom: Fishing boats in port of Alexandria

WHICH QUEENS WERE FAMOUS IN EGYPTIAN HISTORY?

Before the advent of Islam in the seventh century, several women played an important part in the country's history. Hatshepsut, Nefertiti, and Cleopatra are the best known.

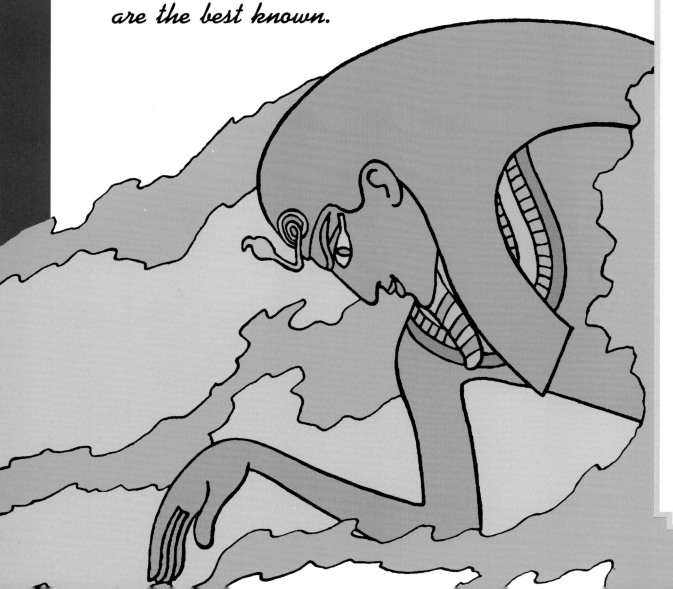

Cleopatra, the wife of the last of the Ptolemy kings, seduced Julius Caesar, then his rival Mark Antony. She was nevertheless unable to prevent Egypt's falling into the hands of Rome after the naval defeat at Actium in 31 B.C. The Roman domination that replaced the Greek influence marked the beginning of a period of unrest. After becoming the jewel of the Roman Empire, then one of the first bastions of Christianity, Egypt wearied of being under the domination of Byzantium, and allowed the armies of the Arab general Omar to invade. In A.D. 642, Egypt became a province of the Islamic Empire. In the tenth century, the Fatimid caliphs made Cairo their wealthy capital, as the Mamelukes did later on.

After Napoleon's brief incursion in 1798, Egypt was governed by viceroys in the name of caliph of Istanbul. Starting with Muhammad Ali, they tried to modernize a country that was partly underdeveloped. The cost of a financial crisis in 1882 enabled Britain to establish its domination over Egypt. Though it became an independent country in 1922, Egypt under the reigns of King Fuad I and then King Farouk had not really freed itself from British control. The gain of power in 1952 of Colonel **Nasser**, who was to become one of the principal leaders of the Arab world, marks the country's real independence. His successors, President **Anwar el-Sadat** in 1970 and President Hosni Mubarak in 1981, have applied themselves primarily to restoring peace among the Arab countries and Israel after the Six-Day War in 1967.

Left: Bas-relief on
the tomb of Ramose in Kerma
Right: The Tomb of Nakht in Kerma

WHO ARE THE COPTS?

Though Egypt has an Islamic majority, it also has a large Christian community, the Copts, who form 5 to 10 percent of the population. Descendants of the people of the pharaohs, Islamics, and Christians live side by side, though not without rivalry and tension.

The church in Egypt was founded at Alexandria by Saint Mark, around A.D. 40. The new religion adopted Coptic, the language of the Egyptian people of the time, and spread rapidly throughout the country despite Roman persecution. Pilgrims came to consult the "desert fathers" who had set up hermitages.

At the time of the Muslim invasion, many Egyptians converted to **Islam** and adopted the Arabic language, but a minority remained faithful to Christianity and to the language of the country. Their name, Copts, is a corruption of the Greek word aiguptos, the first letter of which was not pronounced in Arabic. Often oppressed by the Muslim princes and persecuted by the Mamelukes, who decimated the country's population, the Copts never renounced their faith nor the many customs they have observed for 2,000 years. Christians in Egypt have their own calendar and their own cemeteries, separate from the Muslims'.

The current Egyptian leader, President Mubarak, has adopted a policy of toleration toward all religious groups; but the wave of Islamic **fundamentalism** sweeping Egypt today is making coexistence difficult, rejecting most ideas associated with western civilization, and sometimes making the Copts feel like strangers in their own land.

Top: Copt priest in Atbara (northern Sudan)

Bottom left: Copt monk   Bottom right: Monastery of Wadi Natrun (Lower Egypt)

WHAT IS THE CAPITAL OF EGYPT?

In Arabic, Egypt has had the same name as its capital ever since the time of the caliphs: "Masr," which we know as Cairo. Today it is the largest city in Africa.

Until the Muslim invasion, Cairo was no more than a hamlet on the banks of the Nile. Afterward, and for thirteen centuries, generals, governors of Egypt, Fatimid caliphs, and Mameluke viceroys succeeded each other and made it one of the largest and most beautiful cities in the Arab world. Imposing palaces, hundreds of elegantly minaretted mosques, and colorful souks full of inexhaustible treasures stand side-by-side with fine private houses. Since the end of the nineteenth century, Cairo has become a modern city, with its train stations, underground rail system, and shop-lined thoroughfares, without losing the quaint look of an Asian metropolis, antiquated yet humming with activity.

The intense liveliness contrasts oddly with the funerary monuments surrounding Cairo, from the famous pyramids at Giza, in the western suburbs, to the huge cemeteries extending eastward, where the splendid tombs of Muslim princes alternate with the more modest crypts of the city's inhabitants. The contrast between past splendor and present-day life is striking, all the more so since hundreds of thousands of poor peasants, fleeing the countryside but unable to find housing in this city of 10 million people, have been forced to seek refuge in the cemeteries.

Top: Cairo
Bottom: Woman and child in Cairo

WHERE IS THE WORLD'S LARGEST DESERT?

Located in North Africa, the Sahara extends from the Atlantic coast in the west to the Red Sea in the east. It covers about 3.5 million square miles (9 million sq. km), an area about equal to the United States.

The desert is often imagined as a great expanse covered as far as the eye can see with dunes, sandstorm-sculpted waves. In fact, the dunes cover only 20 percent of the Sahara, a world of infinitely varied landscapes with immense rock-scattered plains (70 percent), mountains carved by erosion (such as Mount Sinai), and even salt crusts originating from the evaporation of freshwater lakes (10 percent). Whether it consists of stones or sand, the desert displays a great variety of colors, from pure white to deepest black, passing through ochre, brown, gray, or mauve, depending on the nature of the rocks.

Contrary to another commonly accepted idea, the desert is not always a synonym for torrid heat: At night, the temperature drops by more than 68°F (20°C), and the winter there, though dry, can be very cold.

It does sometimes rain in the desert, up to 10 inches a year; but the soil, baked by the sun and long periods of drought, absorbs very little of the water. The water flows along on the surface, and to the great surprise of the travelers, makes sudden streams or even veritable rivers—the **wadis**, which disappear as quickly as they rise, carrying away everything in their paths.

Top: The Negev Desert
Bottom: The Nubian Desert

IS THERE ANY LIFE AT ALL IN THE DESERT?

For lack of sufficient moisture, the desert cannot be cultivated. Yet it only appears barren. Real plant and animal life do exist in this seemingly dead territory.

Perfectly adapted to the climate, desert bushes and shrubs absorb water as soon as it rains, and control their evaporation systems as much as possible during periods of drought. These plants have very extensive root systems that allow them to collect water wherever there is the slightest trace of dampness.

Some grasses, whose seeds can survive years of drought, grow as soon as rain has fallen, forming a thin carpet of grass on which scarce gazelles, antelope and migratory birds can be found. The desert is populated with insects, scorpions, and rodents like the graceful **jerboa**. The fennec, or desert fox, is also found there, as well as the jackal, a wild dog. Most of these animals move about only at night, avoiding the intolerable heat of the day. The Arabs, who have always been skillful hunters, train falcons and hawks for hunting, which is considered a noble sport.

In this hostile environment, the oases are veritable islands of coolness, places of permanent water at the surface of the sandy desert. In the shade of the date palms, they shelter small gardens, irrigated by means of a wheel with buckets, called a *noria*, which draws water from a well and distributes it into an astonishing network of channels maintained by oasis inhabitants. Varied in size, oases can support millions of people. They have also served as important links in the caravan trade.

Top: An oasis in Upper Egypt
Bottom left: Water wheel for cleaning water from the Nile

Bottom right:
An Arab prince and his falcon

WHAT IS A BEDOUIN?

Even though the lack of water prevents any agriculture in the desert, some people have nevertheless elected to live there as nomads, driving their flocks from oases to pastures. In Arabia, they are called Bedouin, "the people of the tent."

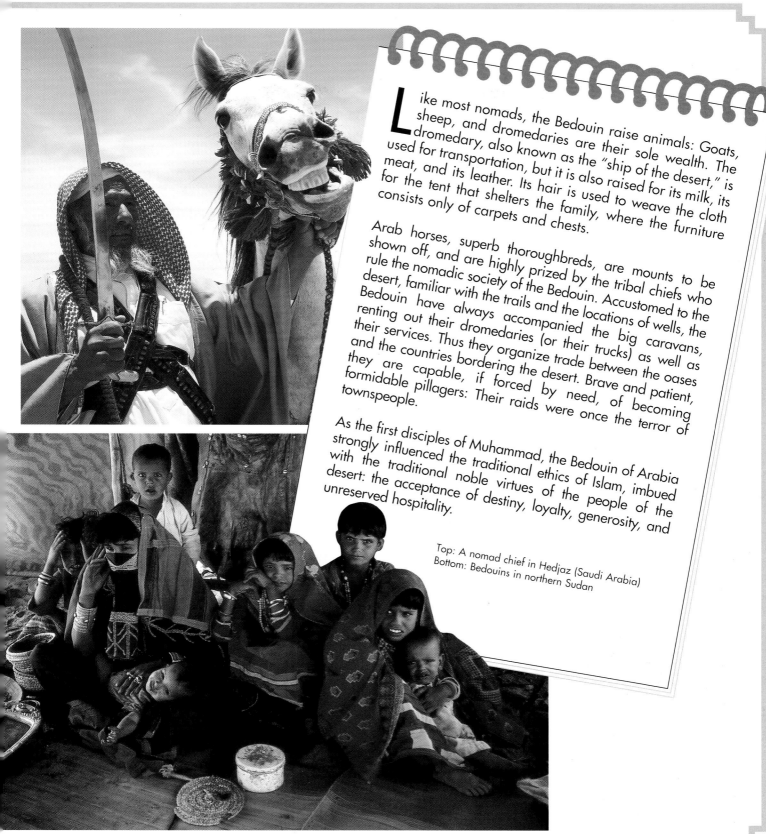

Like most nomads, the Bedouin raise animals: Goats, sheep, and dromedaries are their sole wealth. The dromedary, also known as the "ship of the desert," is used for transportation, but it is also raised for its milk, its meat, and its leather. Its hair is used to weave the cloth for the tent that shelters the family, where the furniture consists only of carpets and chests.

Arab horses, superb thoroughbreds, are mounts to be shown off, and are highly prized by the tribal chiefs who rule the nomadic society of the Bedouin. Accustomed to the desert, familiar with the trails and the locations of wells, the Bedouin have always accompanied the big caravans, renting out their dromedaries (or their trucks) as well as their services. Thus they organize trade between the oases and the countries bordering the desert. Brave and patient, they are capable, if forced by need, of becoming formidable pillagers: Their raids were once the terror of townspeople.

As the first disciples of Muhammad, the Bedouin of Arabia strongly influenced the traditional ethics of Islam, imbued with the traditional noble virtues of the people of the desert: the acceptance of destiny, loyalty, generosity, and unreserved hospitality.

Top: A nomad chief in Hedjaz (Saudi Arabia)
Bottom: Bedouins in northern Sudan

IS ARABIA A COUNTRY?

Arabia, one-third the size of the United States, is a vast peninsula extending from the Red Sea to the Persian Gulf, and from Jordan to the Gulf of Oman. Under the name of Saudi Arabia, it is the largest of the many kingdoms founded by Arabs.

Nomadic shepherds, breeders of dromedaries and horses, or sometimes caravan guides, but also fishermen in coastal areas, tradesmen in the few towns, or farmers in the oases and the mountains, the Arabs have long been divided into a number of tribes. Each tribe still had its chief or **emir**, its dialect, it customs, and its religion. It was only after conversion to Islam and adoption of the language of Muhammad that the Arabs formed a nation and immediately set about the conquest of a huge empire.

The caliphs, or "commanders of the believers," reigned throughout the Middle Ages over an immense territory extending from Spain to northern India. Many countries, have become Muslim, then adopted the Arab language and lifestyle. Thus Egypt and the **Maghreb**, the country of the Berbers, have been part of the "Arab world" ever since, although the majority of their inhabitants are not Arabs by race.

The Arabs, however, formed a number of states that surround Saudi Arabia: Jordan, Syria, and Iraq in the former Fertile Crescent; Yemen and Oman on the south coast, and Kuwait, Qatar, Bahrein, and the United Arab Emirates (a chain of tiny oil-rich kingdoms) along the Persian Gulf. Independent and sometimes rivals to the point of warring with each other, these countries are deeply united when it comes to defending a civilization common to them all.

Top: A fortified village in Yemen
Bottom: A young Arab girl

WHO WAS MUHAMMAD?

Born near Mecca in 570, the prophet Muhammad preached the word of God that he had heard in his meditations. It was only after his death that this revelation was written down in the Koran, which became the sacred book of the Muslims.

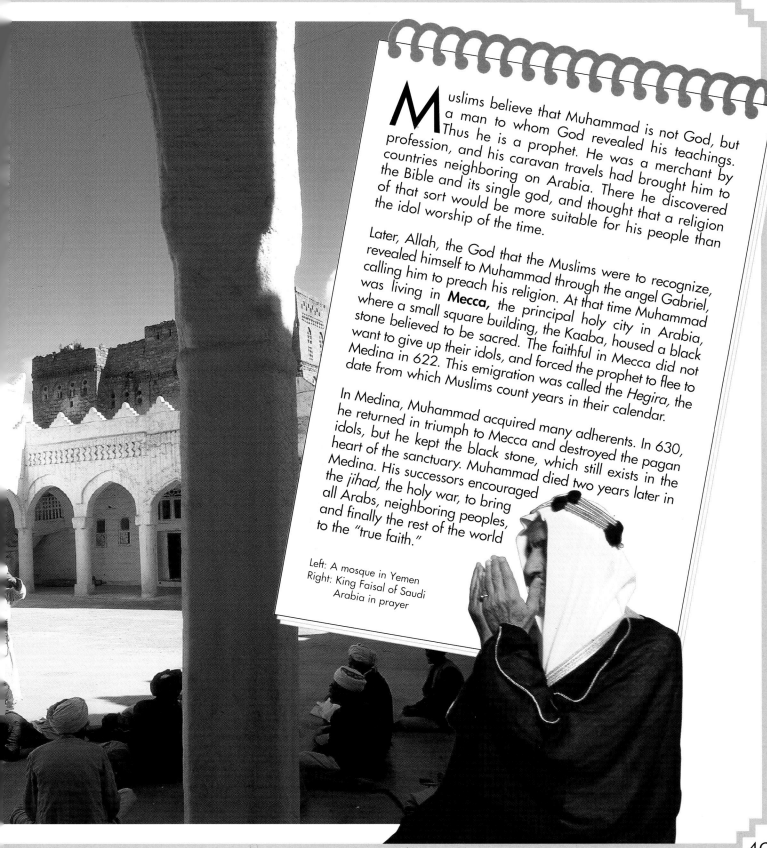

Muslims believe that Muhammad is not God, but a man to whom God revealed his teachings. Thus he is a prophet. He was a merchant by profession, and his caravan travels had brought him to countries neighboring on Arabia. There he discovered the Bible and its single god, and thought that a religion of that sort would be more suitable for his people than the idol worship of the time.

Later, Allah, the God that the Muslims were to recognize, revealed himself to Muhammad through the angel Gabriel, calling him to preach his religion. At that time Muhammad was living in **Mecca,** the principal holy city in Arabia, where a small square building, the Kaaba, housed a black stone believed to be sacred. The faithful in Mecca did not want to give up their idols, and forced the prophet to flee to Medina in 622. This emigration was called the Hegira, the date from which Muslims count years in their calendar.

In Medina, Muhammad acquired many adherents. In 630, he returned in triumph to Mecca and destroyed the pagan idols, but he kept the black stone, which still exists in the heart of the sanctuary. Muhammad died two years later in Medina. His successors encouraged the jihad, the holy war, to bring all Arabs, neighboring peoples, and finally the rest of the world to the "true faith."

Left: A mosque in Yemen
Right: King Faisal of Saudi Arabia in prayer

WHAT MUST A GOOD MUSLIM DO?

In Arabic, Islam means "submission to the divine will." It is the first law of Allah. The Koran specifies the religious duties of Muslims, founded on five main precepts of the Islamic religion.

A ll good Muslims must proclaim in all circumstances the principal article of faith in a single god: "There is no other god but Allah, and Muhammad is his prophet." They must pray five times a day—at dawn, at noon, before and after sunset, and at night, prostrating themselves and facing in the direction of Mecca. These devotions are made in temples called mosques, surmounted by a high tower, the minaret, from which the **muezzin** calls the faithful to prayer.

All good Muslims must fast, in particular in the month of Ramadan, when, for forty days, from sunrise to sunset, they may neither eat nor drink. The Koran also forbids consumption of alcohol and pork meats. All good Muslims must give alms to the poor. At least once in their lifetime, they must perform the *hadj,* the great ritual pilgrimage to Mecca.

These rules, and many other duties or prohibitions, not only dictate private morality but have established a social and political order based on Islamic law, the *charia.* A system of this sort, which only a few Arab countries strictly enforce, does not authorize elections or a parliament to formulate and pass laws. All that counts is the will of Allah, dictated by him in the Koran.

Praying in the Great Mosque of Sanaa

HOW LONG HAVE WE BEEN COUNTING IN "ARABIC" NUMERALS?

In the Middle Ages, Muslim scholars were more advanced than those in the West. That is why the numbers we use today, as well as many inventions and scientific discoveries, came to us then from the Arabs.

The Arab scholars who studied in Alexandria, Baghdad, or Istanbul inherited all the knowledge bequeathed by Antiquity, and they further enriched it as a result of trade contacts with India and China.

The Arabs, great merchants and travelers, needed efficient systems of calculation, especially in astronomy, for their movements on sea and land. Geographical knowledge was also extremely useful for the development of trade and the establishment of diplomatic contacts. Scientists and philosophers enjoyed great prestige. Every prince was eager to have a brilliant court around him, and would sometimes take on as ministers the most celebrated scholars and thinkers of their time. These same princes lavished large amounts of money on the establishment and support of universities where mathematics, astronomy, and medicine were taught.

The **Crusades**, trade in the Mediterranean, and the reconquest of southern Spain from the **Moors** exposed medieval Europe to the immense knowledge accumulated by the Arabs. Our numbers (in which zero is the key to a numbering system much more practical than Roman numbers), and also algebra, the rudiments of chemistry, and astronomy, came to us from the Arabs.

Left: Outdoor classes in arithmetic in the Dakhla oasis

Numbers of the Eastern Arabs

Numbers of the Western Arabs

Numbers in the Twelfth Century

Numbers in the Thirteenth Century

WHAT IS A DHOW?

The dhow is the traditional sailing vessel of Arab fishermen and merchants. The Arabs, who are usually associated with the desert, are also a people of sailors. For over a thousand years, it was the Arabs who dominated maritime trade between the Red Sea and the Indian Ocean.

S inbad the sailor, one of the heroes of **The Thousand and One Nights**, is the incarnation of the courage and enterprising spirit of these long-distance traders who set sail from the ports of Hormuz and Basra in the Persian Gulf, Muscat and Aden on the south coast of Arabia, and Jiddah on the Red Sea.

Throughout the Middle Ages the Arabs, with their knowledge of navigation, launched their dhows from these ports in search of gold, ivory, and slaves (mainly Africans), as well as spices, rare woods, jewelry from India or Java, and silk from China.

Skilled traders, they sold Arabian goods in those countries: incense, myrrh, **gum arabic**, coral, pearls, and horses. Products brought back to Arabia were sold in the **souks**, the trading districts of great cities in the Middle East, still famous for the colorful spectacle they offer, the exotic aromas, and the endless bargaining. Prices were haggled over, while beggars and official inspectors asked for *baksheesh*—alms or tips—still traditional in the modern East.

Left: A sailing ship in Amman
Right: An Arab fishing boat

46

WHY DO MUSLIM WOMEN WEAR A VEIL?

Wearing a veil, imposed on married women by Muhammad, is a sign of purity and modesty. Concealed from the eyes of all but members of her family, the Muslim woman must not attract the glance of other men.

A rab culture attaches great importance to the beauty of women. Muslim poets vie for striking images to praise her charms. In Allah's paradise, houris, women of great beauty, await good Muslims.

The veil, which was falling into disuse in certain countries, is becoming obligatory again under the influence of the fundamentalists. It perpetuates the idea of an unobtrusive role for women in a male-dominated society, respectful of a strict duty of obedience toward their fathers and later their husbands. Although Muslim women are subordinate to men in the eyes of the Koran, they are equal in the eyes of Allah, and have rights against their husbands to protect them from abuse. Polygamy is permitted, but it is becoming less frequent. In the past, the Arab princes and wealthy merchants kept harems, where wives and concubines lived like recluses amid luxury and refinement.

Weddings are one of the most important family occasions, sealing an alliance between two families. Custom requires that the parents of the bride choose the husband and set the amount of the dowry. These festivities are an occasion for great rejoicing and a display of finery.

Left: Sanaa, capital of Yemen   Right: A nomad woman in the Sudan

21

WHAT IS AN ARABESQUE?

Muhammad forbade the representation of God and even of human beings created in his image. So Muslim artists devoted themselves to calligraphy and the creation of abstract decorative designs, called "arabesques."

Calligraphy is the most widespread art in the Muslim world. The beautiful letter forms made it possible to propagate the divine word contained in the Koran, at the same time embellishing it with skillfully drawn designs. It was a golden age for the Arabic alphabet. Calligraphers worked on **parchment** or on paper, which the Arabs imported from China long before the Europeans did. But calligraphy is also found sculpted in stone, on the walls of mosques and of official buildings, executed in glazed earthenware, engraved in wood, or inscribed on copper trays....

The arabesque, the art of decorating with interwoven geometrical designs, inspired by the Greeks and Romans, was pushed to absolute refinement by Arab artists and craftsmen. They applied this type of ornamentation to almost all the materials at their disposal: Morocco gave its name to worked Morocco-leather goods, and "damascening" (designs worked on metal, including copper, came from the city of Damascus, in Syria. The hot climate in their countries induced the Arabs to weave very light fabrics: the fine cottons of Egypt, gauze from Gaza, and muslin from Mosul in Iraq.

Top: An arabesque in Saudi Arabia
Bottom left: Egyptian writing
Bottom right: An arabesque in Yemen

22

WHAT IS ISLAM LIKE TODAY?

Islam, one of the world's great religions, has about 1 billion adherents. But the Arab countries account for only 15 to 20 percent of this community, which is spread over four continents.

The "Arab world" is not to be confused with the "Islamic world." The latter includes populations as diverse as Albanians, Turks, people from sub-Saharan Africa, Iran and Afghanistan, India, Pakistan, Bangladesh, and even Indonesia. The many Muslims living in China or in the republics of the former Soviet Union also belong to this group.

Despite great ethnic diversity, relations that are sometimes very tense among rival movements, such as the **Sunnites** and the **Shiites**, and conflicts among neighboring nations, such as the Iran-Iraq War, Muslims unite as soon as defense of their faith is an issue. Thus they exert a strong influence in today's world. Thanks to the wealth derived from oil production, the Arab countries are playing a leading role in the evolution of the Muslim world, whether the issue is the rejection of domination by Europe or the United States, or the support of the Palestinians' opposition to Israel.

Disappointed by the failure of the Palestinians' armed struggle until the recent peace agreement with Israel, despairing at the slow pace of economic progress and the lack of great Arab figures, the population in several Muslim countries is at present sensitive to a wave of fundamentalism. The return to religious tradition, including within political and social life, and strict application of the charia, the law of the Koran, are subjects increasingly under discussion.

Top: Inside a
        mosque in
        Iraq
Bottom left:
A coffee shop
Bottom right:
A woman from
Amman

23

WHAT IS "BLACK GOLD"?

In former times Arabia was well known for its spices and its perfumes. Today, thanks to oil, the Middle East has become one of the richest regions in the world.

In ancient times, a distinction used to be made between "desert Arabia" and "lucky Arabia," a country where plants grew with perfumes more precious than gold: incense, myrrh, rose, and jasmin, then unknown in Europe. Purple and indigo were also much in demand for dyeing fabrics.

Fruit was equally well appreciated, and every region was known for its specialty: dates in Iraq, apples in Syria, plums in Damascus, figs in Jerusalem, peaches and apricots in Iran. Later on, it was also through these countries that Europe was to discover oranges, artichokes, and spinach, while the whole world adopted a little red bean from the high plateaus of Yemen—coffee! Today, the Near East derives most of its wealth from oil, formerly used as a medicinal tincture or a lamp fuel, but after the invention of the combustion engine, as a motor fuel.

The first oil-producing countries, Iran, Iraq, Saudi Arabia, and the emirates in the Persian Gulf, have control over fabulous wealth. This power is too often used, unfortunately to purchase arms or to sustain the excessive luxury of a few princely families.

Left: Oil well in Ain Dar, Saudi Arabia
Right: A Bedouin from Abu Dhabi

24

WHO INVENTED WRITING?

Over 5,000 years ago, the Sumerians in Mesopotamia founded the first of a series of brilliant civilizations. Builders of great cities and skillful farmers, they also invented writing, which marks the beginning of recorded history.

Mesopotamia, whose name in Greek means "between two rivers," is appropriately named. Indeed, it is a huge plain located between the Tigris and Euphrates rivers. As in Egypt, this fertile region was cultivated very early; the population became prosperous and large enough to found cities full of merchants, craftsmen, physicians, and priests well versed in astrology. Their knowledge, engraved on clay tablets, reached us thanks to a writing called **cuneiform.** The writing of wedge-shaped characters was done by pressing a nail-like stylus onto tablets of unhardened clay, that when dried in the sun, retained the imprint indefinitely.

The fact that our minutes and seconds are counted by 60 is due to the calculations of Sumerian astronomers, while their successors, the Chaldeans, bequeathed us the seven-day week. For twenty-five centuries Mesopotamia continued to be an important center of civilization. Coming out of the Arabian desert, the Akkadians and then the Assyrians made Babylon a city famous beyond all others, and the names of their kings are still celebrated: Hammurabi, Nebuchadnezzar, Ashurbanipal, and Queen Semiramis.

After 1,000 years of Persian domination, a new capital again made this area one of the centers of the world, when the Muslim caliphs settled in Baghdad and reigned there for five centuries. The most famous of them, Harun ar-Rashid, is known to us through the tales of *The Thousand and One Nights.*

Top: The ancient village of Assur in Mesopotamia (Iraq)
Bottom: Cuneiform writing

25

WHO WERE THE PHOENICIANS?

The Phoenicians were a desert people who settled 3,000 years ago on the coast of present-day Lebanon. It is to them that we owe the alphabet.

Tyre, built on the island where the shellfish were found from which **purple** dye was derived; Sidon, where glass used to be blown; and Byblos, famous for its papyrus, were the great ports of the Phoenicians. This people had constructed sophisticated vessels, propelled by oars and sails, that took its mariners to Egypt, Greece, and Spain. From the Strait of Gibraltar, they ventured as far afield as Cornwall, in the south of present-day England, to purchase the tin ore used in making bronze.

Sharp-witted merchants, the Phoenicians adapted the cuneiform writing invented by the Sumerians to use for their accounts. The alphabet of 22 symbols that they perfected, transmitted to the Greeks and then to the Romans, who increased it to 26 symbols, is the same one that we still use today.

Rich and powerful, but poor warriors, the Phoenicians eventually yielded to the Roman legions and disappeared as a nation. Their most important colony, Carthage, on the Tunisian coast, resisted for a long time, however, under the direction of a brave general, Hannibal. And when the Roman consuls sent word to Rome of their victory, they were using, probably unknowingly, a Phoenician invention—the alphabet!

Left: Tyre, Phoenician archeological site in Lebanon

Right: The head of Sargon of Akkad (Mesopotamia, c. 2350 B.C.)

26

WHICH COUNTRY WAS CALLED THE "SWITZERLAND OF THE EAST"?

Until 1946, Lebanon was called the "Switzerland of the East" because of its role as a center of Mediterranean trade, and because of the peaceful coexistence of Christians and Muslims.

In Lebanon, the geography divides different population groups. High mountain ranges separate the coastal plains, inhabited by Christians since the time of the Phoenicians, from the valleys of the interior, peopled by Arabs who came from the desert. The political system has made room for each of these communities, traditionally dominated by "barons," or heads of wealthy and respected great families.

At the time of the creation of the **State of Israel**, the fragile balance in Lebanon was upset by the arrival of many Palestinian refugees. Encouraged by the Arab countries, especially by Syria, of which Lebanon had formerly been part for a long time, the Palestinians set up a veritable state within a state, and created their own army in opposition to Israel. From 1950 on, but especially in 1975 and 1989, the various communities, each with its unofficial army, clashed in a merciless civil war that ravaged the country and its capital, Beirut, decimating the population with horrendous massacres.

Today, Lebanon, which is theoretically independent but in reality divided between Israel and Syria, is assessing its situation and mourning its dead. The disagreement between Jews and Arabs, who are struggling to establish peace, still disturbs the region, which could be torn apart by war at any time.

Top: Mountains in Lebanon
Bottom: A Lebanese farmer from the Bekaa Valley

60

61

27

WHY IS JERUSALEM THREE TIMES HOLY?

Though Jerusalem, the capital of Israel, is the biblical city of the Jews, it is also a holy city for Christians and Muslims.

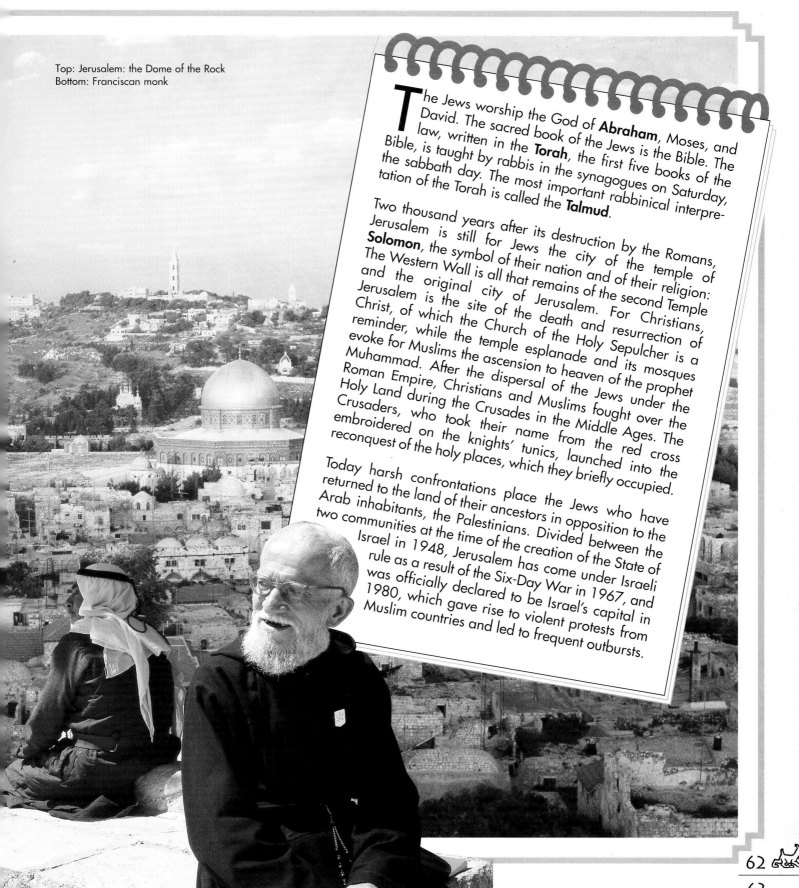

Top: Jerusalem: the Dome of the Rock
Bottom: Franciscan monk

The Jews worship the God of **Abraham**, Moses, and David. The sacred book of the Jews is the Bible. The law, written in the **Torah**, the first five books of the Bible, is taught by rabbis in the synagogues on Saturday, the sabbath day. The most important rabbinical interpretation of the Torah is called the **Talmud**.

Two thousand years after its destruction by the Romans, Jerusalem is still for Jews the city of the temple of **Solomon**, the symbol of their nation and of their religion: The Western Wall is all that remains of the second Temple and the original city of Jerusalem. For Christians, Jerusalem is the site of the death and resurrection of Christ, of which the Church of the Holy Sepulcher is a reminder, while the temple esplanade and its mosques evoke for Muslims the ascension to heaven of the prophet Muhammad. After the dispersal of the Jews under the Roman Empire, Christians and Muslims fought over the Holy Land during the Crusades in the Middle Ages. The Crusaders, who took their name from the red cross embroidered on the knights' tunics, launched into the reconquest of the holy places, which they briefly occupied.

Today harsh confrontations place the Jews who have returned to the land of their ancestors in opposition to the Arab inhabitants, the Palestinians. Divided between the two communities at the time of the creation of the State of Israel in 1948, Jerusalem has come under Israeli rule as a result of the Six-Day War in 1967, and was officially declared to be Israel's capital in 1980, which gave rise to violent protests from Muslim countries and led to frequent outbursts.

28

HAVE JEWS ALWAYS LIVED IN ISRAEL?

Often dominated, deported, or oppressed by conquering peoples, most Jews left their country of origin at the beginning of the Christian era. Some Jews remained in Israel, however, even if in small numbers. It was not until after World War II that Jews returned to found a new Israel.

The twelve tribes of the Hebrew people, who had come from the desert 3,500 years before, founded Israel in the land of Canaan, the "Promised Land" in Palestine. But this region, fought over by the powerful empires of Egypt and Assyria, was inhabited by other peoples, too: the Aramaeans, the Philistines, and the Samaritans. Thus the Hebrews had a troubled history during the biblical period, despite the strong and unified rules of Saul, David, and Solomon. Shortly after the time of Christ, persecution by the Romans caused the Hebrews to scatter to the four corners of the world: This was known as the *diaspora*.

Merchants, craftsmen, or bankers in the cities, but peasants as well, the Jews were often rejected by Christians and Muslims. They were driven out of some countries, herded into **ghettos** in others, massacred in the pogroms of Russia, and mass-murdered in Nazi concentration camps in the **Holocaust** of World War II.

These terrible ordeals accentuated the desire of the Jewish people to return to the land of their ancestors. A movement was formed known as Zionism, from Zion, another name for Jerusalem. From the 1880s but mainly after 1945, the movement encouraged Jews around the world to return to Palestine and found their state there. In 1948, hundreds of thousands of Jews left Europe or North Africa and the Middle East and returned to Palestine to create the present State of Israel. The Zionist movement conflicted with the Palestinian's view of their homeland.

Top: Reading the Torah
Bottom: The Western Wall in Jerusalem

29

DO THE PALESTINIANS HAVE A COUNTRY OF THEIR OWN?

Arabs had come to settle in Palestine after the departure of the Jews, and a large number of Palestinian Arabs fled their country at the time of the creation of the State of Israel, taking refuge in Jordan, Lebanon, and various other Arab countries.

The Palestinians, who for a long time had outnumbered the few Jews remaining in Palestine, were eventually overwhelmed by the influx of Jewish settlers who ran from the Nazis in the 1930s. Many of the Jewish settlers were able to buy land helped by contributions from Jews all over the world. The Jewish settlers developed their properties and founded small farming communities, the *kibbutzim*. The Arab countries, emotionally attached to the land, turned down all proposals by Britain and by the UNO for sharing the country between Jews and Arabs. As a result, the Palestinians were at war against Israel from the time it was created in 1948. After a series of conflicts, the Israeli army eventually occupied both parts of Palestine, Cisjordan and the Gaza area, set aside for the Arabs by the UNO.

The Arabs, like the Christian Palestinians who had stayed on, responded to Israeli domination with riots and terrorist actions, and formed a number of different organizations. The largest is the PLO (Palestinian Liberation Organization), with Yassir Arafat as leader. Despite the peace concluded in 1978 at **Camp David** between President Anwar Sadat of Egypt and Prime Minister Menachim Begin of Israel, the coexistence of Jews and Arabs in this part of the world remains very conflictive. In 1993, an agreement between Israel and the PLO returned Jericho and the Gaza strip to an autonomous Palestinian rule.

Left: An entrance to the mosque at Omar
Right: A Palestinian

30

HOW DID THE DEAD SEA GET ITS NAME?

Surrounded by torrid deserts and subject to a high rate of evaporation, the Dead Sea today has hardly any water left in it. Its salt content is so high that even fish cannot live there.

The Dead Sea is a closed and collapsed basin between faults in which the river Jordan flows and evaporates. It is the lowest level of water in the world. Gorged with salt and also with sulphur and bitumen that spread along its banks, the water of the Dead Sea has a taste that is detestable to both animals and human beings. Its salts and minerals are mined individually for agricultural fertilizers. It is so dense that the human body cannot sink, but floats on the surface instead.

And yet these sterile landscapes, between the Negev and Nafud deserts near the borders of Israel and Jordan, have not always been uninhabited. Around the time of Christ, the Jewish sect of the Essenes had taken refuge in caves along the shore. Recently their sacred books were discovered there: the famous **"Dead Sea Scrolls"** which enabled archeologists to reveal hitherto unknown variants of the Bible, and to evaluate its events.

In these regions, religious retreats into the depths of the desert are traditional. Jesus himself withdrew into it for 40 days, according to the Gospel. The custom is as persistent among Christians in the East as it is among Muslims. Distant heirs of the Desert Fathers, some anchorites ("those who keep apart") still withdraw today to meditate and pray in the desert in Egypt or in Sinai, not far from the Dead Sea. Thus the monks of Saint Catherine's monastery have lived for fifteen centuries on the slopes of Mount Sinai, the holy mountain where Moses received from God the Ten Commandments respected by the three great monotheistic religions—Judaism, Christianity, and Islam.

A

ABRAHAM : biblical patriarch. He is the father of Isaac, who is the father of Jacob. Through his sons, Ismail, whose mother, Agar, is Arab, and Isaac, whose mother, Sarah, is Jewish, he appears according to tradition as the ancestor of Arabs and Jews.

ANWAR EL-SADAT (1918–1981) : president of Egypt from 1970 until his death. He was responsible for negotiating the return of land from Israel and for signing an historic peace agreement with Israel after talks at Camp David with Prime Minister Menachim Begin of Israel and President Jimmy Carter of the United States. Sadat and Begin were awarded the Nobel Peace Prize in 1978.

ASWAN HIGH DAM : near the first Nile falls in Upper Egypt. An artificial lake was created first in 1902 by the British. A huge dam, begun in 1956 and completed in 1970, was built with Soviet aid about 4 miles (6.5 km) upstream. It holds over 150 billion cubic meters of water, of which one-sixth is lost to evaporation.

C

CHAMPOLLION (JEAN-FRANCOIS) (1790– 1832) : French founder of Egyptology. The text of the Rosetta Stone, composed in hieroglyphics, and that of a fresco on Philai led him to decipher ancient Egyptian writing.

CAMP DAVID : located in Maryland, the official retreat of the President of the United States. In 1978 President Carter of the United States held meetings here with Prime Minister Begin of Israel and President Sadat of Egypt to sign a peace treaty to reduce tensions between Israel and Egypt in a step toward stability in the Middle East.

CRUSADES (1095–1291) : expeditions undertaken by coalitions of Christians to deliver the Holy Lands that were occupied by the Muslims.

CUNEIFORM : "in the shape of a wedge." Writing made up of various combinations of wedge-shaped symbols.

D

DEAD SEA SCROLLS : manuscripts discovered in 1947 (Qumran Caves) that constitute the library of the Essenes and make it possible to understand the life of the community and its doctrine. The oldest known Bible documents (second century B.C.) were found in them.

E

EGYPTOLOGY : study of Egyptian antiquity.

EMIR : honorary title given to heads of the Muslim world: princes, governors, military chiefs.

F

FERTILE CRESCENT : narrow strip of land shaped like the segment of an arc starting from the east of the Mediterranean (Israel–Lebanon), widening toward the north (Syria), then turning southeast (Tigris and Euphrates plains, in Iraq) to link up with the Persian Gulf. The name, mainly historical, refers to the powerful empires of Babylonia, Assyria, and Phoenicia.

FUNDAMENTALISM : attitude of religious groups who profess belief in tradition and refuse any evolution; the rejection of modernization by many Islamic societies.

G

GHETTO : section of a city where Jews were forced to live apart from the rest of the population. Today the term applies to a section of a city where any minority group lives because of social, legal, or economic pressure.

GUM ARABIC : derived from various species of acacia from hot desert regions, it is water-soluable and used to make medicines, perfumes, candies, and mucilage.

H

HATSHEPSUT (1505–1484 B.C.) : seventeenth dynasty queen of Egypt. She followed a pacifist policy and had the famous terraced temple built at Deir el-Bahari. After her death, Thutmose III persecuted her memory and had her name removed from all monuments.

HOLOCAUST : The mass slaughter of European civilians, especially Jews, by the Nazis during World War II.

I

ISLAM : name of the religion preached by Muhammad. Its adherents are called Muslims.

J

JERBOA : small rodent with very short front legs, very long back feet and tail, which enable it to stand upright like a kangaroo and to leap.

M

MAGHREB : "place of the setting sun." Name given to all of North Africa contained between the Mediterranean and the Sahara, the Atlantic Ocean and Libya.

MARIETTE (AUGUST) (1821–1881) : French Egyptologist who, in 1858, was the first conservator of the Egyptian Monuments, and whose discoveries became the core of the famous Egyptian Museum in Cairo.

MECCA : Islam's largest pilgrimage center. The city, birthplace of the prophet Muhammad, is forbidden to non-Muslims.

MESOPOTAMIA : from the Greek *mesos* (middle) and *potamos* (river), a huge area comprising the valleys of the Tigris and the Euphrates rivers. Cradle of the Sumerian-Akkadian civilization, it constitutes the greater part of present-day Iraq.

MOORS : presently the populations of the western Sahara living in Mauritania. For a long time the name designated, in the West, the Berbers, in particular the conquerors of Spain.

MUEZZIN : a Muslim religious official attached to a mosque, whose function is to call the faithful to prayer from the minaret.

N

NASSER (GAMAL ABDEL) (1918–1970) : president of Egypt from 1956 to 1970, he seized power from King Faruk in 1952. He nationalized the Suez Canal in 1956, causing a diplomatic crisis, formed a short-lived union with Syria as the United Arab Republic, fought for nationalism, economic reform, and improved education. His aim was to unite all Arabs under Egyptian leadership, and he took the first steps toward peace with Israel.

NATRON : crystallized natural sodium carbonate.

NEFERTITI : during the second half of the fourteenth century B.C., she was Queen of Egypt and wife of Pharaoh Amenophis IV, known as Akhenaton. She took part in the religious revolution achieved by her husband, and remained faithful to the cult of Aton after his death.

O

OBELISK : raised stone in the shape of a four-sided needle with a pyramid-shaped top. Obelisks presented as gifts from Egypt can be found in New York City, London, Paris, and Rome.

P

PARCHMENT : animal skin (of sheep, lamb, or goat) specially prepared to be written on.

PHARAOH : a name given by the Hebrews to describe the king of Egypt. It originally was the Egyptian word for royal residence.

S

SCRIBE : essential Egyptian government official, whose task was to read and write down governmental, religious, and juridicial acts.

SHIITE : meaning "on Ali's side," a political Arab movement that contested the legality of the prophet's succession advantageous to Abu-Bakr and detrimental to Ali, cousin and adopted son of Muhammad.

SOLOMON (c. 972–931 B.C.) : king of Israel, son of David and Bathsheba. His reign marks the high point of Israel's power.

SOUK : covered market with small shops and workshops in a tangle of little streets.

STATE OF ISRAEL : the result of Jewish immigration to Palestine. The General Assembly of the United Nations voted in November 1947 to divide the country into two states, one Arab and one Jewish. This was accepted by the Jewish leaders and rejected by the Arabs. Israel officially came into existence on May 14, 1948.

STELA : Greek word for a pillar or vertical tablet that contained inscriptions or decorations in relief.

SUNNITE : follower of "sunna" tradition. A Muslim who considers himself orthodox compared to the Shiites.

T

TALMUD : a collection of writings on law and history that serves as a guide to the practice of Judaism.

"THE THOUSAND AND ONE NIGHTS" : a collection of Arabian tales.

TORAH : a Hebrew word meaning "doctrine," "law," it is the name given to the first five books of the Bible, the Law of Moses (Pentateuch). The text is hand-written by scribes on a roll of parchment that is wound around two wooden rods.

TUTANKHAMEN (1354 B.C.) : eighteenth dynasty pharaoh, the son-in-law of Amenophis IV, whom he succeeded when very young. He abolished the worship of Aton and reestablished the official religion. He died at the age of 20 after a reign about which little is known. His tomb, discovered in 1922 in the Valley of the Kings, is one of the very few whose treasures have been saved.

U

UNESCO : United Nations Educational, Scientific, and Cultural Organization.

W

WADI : Arabic word meaning "water course" or "river" in North Africa. Temporary water course in arid regions.

chronology

B.C.
4000

First cities, Sumerian (Mesopotamian) temples, cuneiform writing (c. 3700)
The first pharaohs unify Egypt (c. 3100)
Appearance of hieroglyphs (c. 3100)

3000

Megalithic buildings at Stonehenge, England (2686–2181)

Construction of the great pyramids (c. 2800–1500)

2000

Beginning of the Bronze Age (c. 2000)
Construction of the Valley of the Kings at Thebes (1500–1100)
Jewish exodus from Egypt (c. 1200)

Mycenae was leading political and cultural center of Greece (1400–1200)

1000

The Assyrians destroy Babylon (689)
Egypt falls to the Arabs (639)
Alexander the Great founds Alexandria in Egypt (332)
Defeat of Cleopatra, who surrenders Egypt to the Roman Empire (30)

Democracy is born in Athens (461)

0

Jews are expelled from Jerusalem—beginning of the *diaspora* (135)

Fall of Rome (476)

500

Death of Muhammad (632)
Egypt falls to the Arabs (639)
Islam split between Sunnites and Shiites (657)
Fatimite caliphate establishes rule in Egypt—sets up capital in Cairo (969)

Muslims defeated near Tours (732), stopping the spread of Islam into Western Europe.

1000

Capture of Jerusalem by the Crusaders (1099)

The Crusades begin (1096)
Marco Polo travels in China (1271–1295)
Columbus sets sail for the Americas (1492)

1500

Napoleon's Egyptian campaign (1798)
Construction of the Suez Canal (1858–1869)

The American Revolution begins (1776)
French Revolution (1789)

1900
A.D.

Founding of the State of Israel (1948)
Nasser comes to power in Egypt (1954)
Israel invades the Sinai Peninsula (1956)
Construction of the Aswan High Dam (1960–1971)
Iraq invades Kuwait (1990)
Palestinian-Israeli Accord (1993)

Holocaust of European Jews under Hitler (1942–1945)

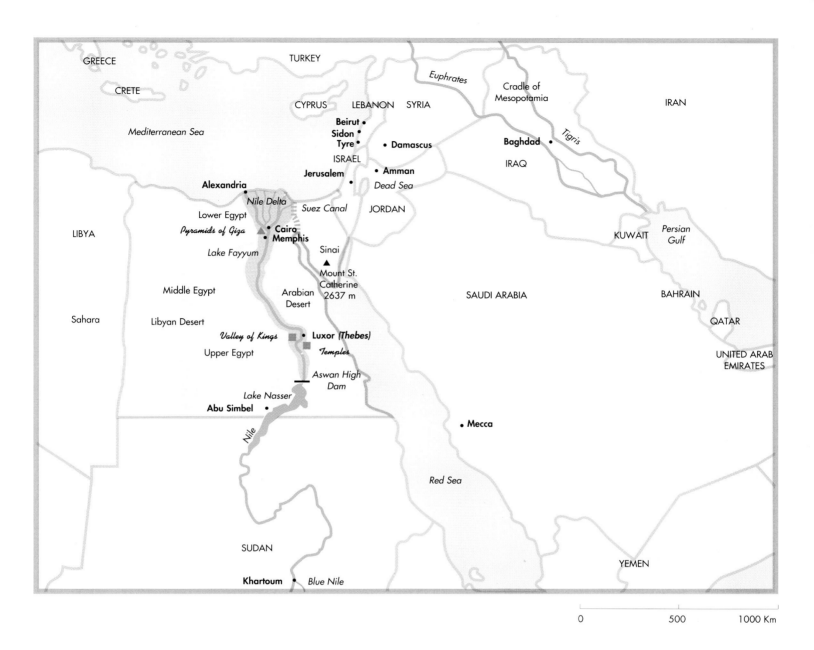

GREECE

TURKEY

CRETE

CYPRUS   LEBANON   SYRIA

Euphrates

Cradle of
Mesopotamia

IRAN

Beirut
Sidon
Tyre

• **Damascus**

Baghdad •

Tigris

Mediterranean Sea

ISRAEL

Jerusalem

• **Amman**

IRAQ

Alexandria

Nile Delta

Dead Sea

Suez Canal

JORDAN

Lower Egypt

Pyramids of Giza

• **Cairo**
• **Memphis**

KUWAIT

*Persian
Gulf*

LIBYA

Lake Fayyum

Sinai

*Mount St.
Catherine
2637 m*

SAUDI ARABIA

BAHRAIN

Middle Egypt

Arabian
Desert

QATAR

Sahara

Libyan Desert

Valley of Kings

Upper Egypt

▢ • **Luxor (Thebes)**
▢
Temples

UNITED ARAB
EMIRATES

*Aswan High
Dam*

Lake Nasser

Abu Simbel •

Nile

• **Mecca**

Red Sea

SUDAN

YEMEN

Khartoum   *Blue Nile*

0   500   1000 Km

EGYPT

Capital: Cairo
Area: 386,662 sq. miles (1,001,449 sq. km)
Population: 57,082,000

index

bibliography

EGYPT AND THE MIDDLE EAST, FOR READERS FROM 7 TO 77

Aldred, Cyril.
Egyptian Art in the Days of the Pharaohs.
New York: Oxford University Press, 1980.

Atil, Esin.
Renaissance of Islam: Art of the Mamluks.
Washington, D.C.: Smithsonian Institution Press, 1981.

Cohen, Daniel.
Ancient Egypt.
New York: Doubleday, 1989.

Crosher, Judith.
Ancient Egypt.
New York: Viking, 1993.

Cross, Wilbur.
Egypt.
Chicago: Childrens Press, 1982.

Edwards, Iowerth.
The Pyramids of Egypt.
New York: Penguin Books, 1985.

Esposito, John L.
Islam: The Straight Path.
New York: Oxford University Press, 1988.

Feinstein, Steve.
Egypt—In Pictures.
Minneapolis: Lerner Publications Co., 1988.

Gordon, Matthew.
Islam.
New York: Facts on File, 1991.

Glubok, Shirley.
The Mummy of Ramose: The Life and Death of an Ancient Egyptian Nobleman.
New York: Harper & Row, 1978.

Harris, Geraldine.
Ancient Egypt.
New York: Facts on File, 1990.

James, Thomas Garnet Henry.
Pharaoh's People: Scenes From Life In Imperial Egypt.
Chicago: University of Chicago Press, 1981.

Khan, Muhammad Zafrulla.
Muhammad, Seal of the Prophets.
Boston: Routledge & Kegan Paul, 1980.

Koenig, Viviane.
The Ancient Egyptians: Life in the Nile Valley.
Brookfield, CT, Millbrook Press, 1992.

Lewis, Bernard.
Islam and the West.
New York: Oxford University Press, 1993.

Lippman, Thomas W.
Egypt After Nasser: Sadat, Peace, and the Mirage of Prosperity.
New York: Paragon House, 1989.

Marston, Elsa.
Lebanon.
Dillon: Silver Burdett, 1991.

Naden, Corinne J.
The Nile River.
New York: Watts, 1972.

Nutting, Anthony.
Nasser.
New York: E. P. Dutton, 1972.

Perl, Lila.
Egypt: Rebirth On the Nile.
New York: Morrow, 1977.

Putnam, Jim.
Mummy.
New York: A. A. Knopf, 1993.

Rossi, Guido Alberto.
Egypt: Gift of the Nile: An Aerial Portrait.
New York: H. N. Abrams, 1992.

Smith, William Stevenson.
The Art and Architecture of Ancient Egypt.
New York: Penguin Books, 1981.

Warren, Ruth.
The Nile: The Story of Pharaoh, Farmers and Explorers.
New York: McGraw-Hill, 1968.

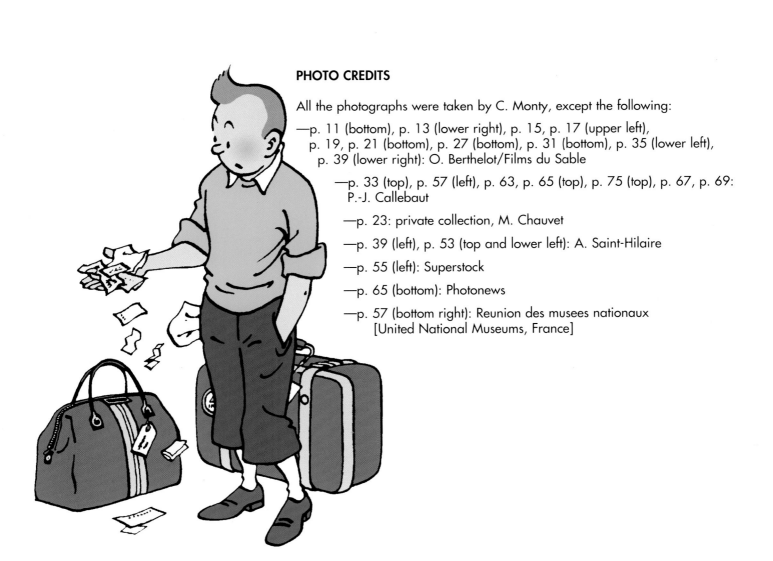

PHOTO CREDITS

All the photographs were taken by C. Monty, except the following:

—p. 11 (bottom), p. 13 (lower right), p. 15, p. 17 (upper left),
p. 19, p. 21 (bottom), p. 27 (bottom), p. 31 (bottom), p. 35 (lower left),
p. 39 (lower right): O. Berthelot/Films du Sable

—p. 33 (top), p. 57 (left), p. 63, p. 65 (top), p. 75 (top), p. 67, p. 69:
P.-J. Callebaut

—p. 23: private collection, M. Chauvet

—p. 39 (left), p. 53 (top and lower left): A. Saint-Hilaire

—p. 55 (left): Superstock

—p. 65 (bottom): Photonews

—p. 57 (bottom right): Reunion des musees nationaux
[United National Museums, France]

Titles in the *Tintin's Travel Diaries* series: